JR. GRAPHIC MONSTER STORIES

BIGFOOT!

STEVEN ROBERTS

PowerKiDS press

New York

Published in 2013 by The Rosen Publishing Group, Inc.
29 East 21st Street, New York, NY 10010

First Edition

Editor: Joanne Randolph
Book Design: Planman Technologies
Illustrations: Planman Technologies

Library of Congress Cataloging-in-Publication Data

Roberts, Steven.
 Bigfoot! / By Steven Roberts.
    p. cm. — (Jr. graphic monster stories)
Includes index.
ISBN 978-1-4488-7901-4 (library binding) — ISBN 978-1-4488-8001-0 (pbk.) —
ISBN 978-1-4488-8007-2 (6-pack)
1. Sasquatch. 1. Title.
QL89.2.S2R63 2012
001.944—dc23

                                        2012002150

Manufactured in the United States of America

CPSIA Compliance Information: Batch # SW12PK: For Further Information contact Rosen Publishing,
New York, New York at 1-800-237-9932

Contents

Main Characters

Fred Beck (c. 1920s) A miner who, with his friends, was **attacked** by a group of "ape men" in 1924 in Ape Canyon near Mt. St. Helens, Washington.

Jerry Crew (c. 1950s) Bulldozer operator who, in 1958, made a copy of a large bigfoot footprint at a job site near Bluff Creek, California.

Roger Patterson and Robert Gimlin (c. 1960s) In 1967, they made a famous film of a female bigfoot in a remote area near Bluff Creek, California.

Bigfoot Facts and Figures

- Bigfoot creatures have been known by many different names. These include "hairy man," "ape man," "forest creature," "timber giant," and "Sasquatch."

- Bigfoot has been described as being up to 8 feet (2 m) tall and weighing as much as 500 pounds (227 kg). It is said to have the general stature of a man but with long arms and a short neck. People say bigfoot has long, brown hair that covers its entire body. Its huge footprints can be almost 2 feet (61 cm) long and 8 to 10 inches (20-25 cm) wide. It is thought that bigfoot is **nocturnal**.

- Stories about bigfoot were part of Native American **folklore** long before Europeans came to North America. In the 1800s, the American **missionary** Elkanah Walker recorded some of these **legends**. He wrote that Native Americans from the Spokane, Washington, area told stories of giants who lived at the top of mountains. They came down from the mountains at night to steal salmon from fishermen's nets.

Bigfoot!

TONY AND MARIO WERE BACKPACKING IN THE WOODS OF THE PACIFIC NORTHWEST.

THIS LOOKS LIKE A GOOD PLACE TO SET UP CAMP.

MARIO HEARD SOMETHING IN THE WOODS.

DID YOU HEAR THAT?

HEAR WHAT?

THE TWO MEN COULD NOT BELIEVE THEIR EYES.

DID YOU SEE WHAT I JUST SAW?

I THINK THAT WAS BIGFOOT!

WE SHOULD FOLLOW IT AND GET A PICTURE!

I'M NOT GOING NEAR THAT THING. DID YOU SEE HOW BIG IT IS?

6

"A MAN NAMED FRED BECK WAS MINING FOR GOLD IN THE CANYON WITH SOME FRIENDS.

"SUDDENLY, A LARGE CREATURE APPEARED NEARBY. BECK LATER DESCRIBED IT AS AN 'APE MAN.'"

GROWWWWL

WHAT IS THAT?

DON'T MOVE OR IT MIGHT ATTACK!

"BECK'S FRIEND HANK GRABBED HIS RIFLE. HE TOOK A SHOT AT THE CREATURE BUT MISSED."

POW!

CRACK!

"BECK AND HIS FRIENDS RAN BACK TO THE CABIN AND BOLTED THE DOOR. THEY DECIDED TO LEAVE THE CANYON FIRST THING IN THE MORNING."

WE'LL HAVE TO SPEND THE NIGHT HERE. IT'S TOO DANGEROUS TO TRAVEL IN THE DARK.

"THEY DID THEIR BEST TO GET SOME SLEEP THAT NIGHT."

"SOON, THE MEN HEARD A LOUD NOISE."

CRASH!

GET UP! IT IS THE APE MAN!

"BIGFOOT MOVED AWAY FROM THE CABIN. BECK RAN OVER TO LOOK OUT THE WINDOW AND SAW SEVERAL OF THE STRANGE CREATURES OUTSIDE.

"BECK QUICKLY REALIZED THEY WERE ABOUT TO BE ATTACKED."

SMASH!

WE ARE IN TROUBLE.

"THE ATTACK WENT ON THROUGHOUT THE NIGHT."

POW!

AAAAARGH!

HOLD THE DOOR!

"THE MEN KEPT THE BIGFOOTS FROM GETTING INSIDE THE CABIN THAT NIGHT. IN THE MORNING, THE BIGFOOTS WERE GONE. BECK AND HIS FRIENDS FLED AS FAST AS THEY COULD."

LET'S GET OUT OF HERE!

"THEY REPORTED WHAT THEY HAD SEEN TO THE LOCAL SHERIFF."

THEY WERE THIS BIG!

THEY TRIED TO KILL US!

"THE SHERIFF HIKED TO THE CABIN WITH THE THREE MEN. IT HAD RAINED HEAVILY SO THERE WERE NO FOOTPRINTS. THEY APPROACHED THE BATTERED CABIN."

YOU GUYS FOUGHT AND TORE THE PLACE UP, DIDN'T YOU? YOU ARE LUCKY I DON'T THROW YOU IN JAIL!

HAS ANYONE EVER BEEN ABLE TO PROVE THAT BIGFOOT REALLY EXISTS?

WELL, PEOPLE HAVE COME UP WITH A LITTLE EVIDENCE.

"IN 1958, A CONSTRUCTION CREW WAS CLEARING SOME LAND IN NORTHERN CALIFORNIA.

"A WORKER NAMED JERRY CREW FOUND SOME STRANGE FOOTPRINTS.

"CREW KNEW THAT NO ONE WOULD BELIEVE HIM IF HE TOLD THEM ABOUT THE FOOTPRINTS, SO HE MADE A **PLASTER CAST** OF ONE OF THEM."

THEY'LL BELIEVE ME NOW.

"HE TOOK THE CAST OF THE FOOTPRINT TO A LOCAL NEWSPAPER. THE NEWSPAPER PRINTED A PHOTO OF IT."

THAT FOOTPRINT PHOTO CAUSED A NATIONAL **SENSATION.** IT WAS HOW BIGFOOT GOT ITS NAME.

13

IS THAT THE ONLY PROOF? JUST A FOOTPRINT?

NO. A COUPLE OF GUYS ACTUALLY CAUGHT BIGFOOT ON FILM.

"IN 1967, ROGER PATTERSON AND ROBERT GIMLIN HEARD ABOUT A BIGFOOT IN BLUFF CREEK, CALIFORNIA, AND SET OUT TO FIND IT.

"THEY CAME ACROSS A BIGFOOT CROUCHED DOWN NEXT TO A LARGE OVERTURNED TREE.

"THEY QUICKLY GOT OFF THEIR HORSES AND TOOK OUT THEIR CAMERA.

"THEIR FILM BECAME WORLD FAMOUS. IT IS THE CLOSEST ANYONE HAS COME TO PROVING BIGFOOT IS REAL.

"IN 2007, A HUNTER TOOK A PICTURE OF WHAT HE THOUGHT WAS BIGFOOT."

OVER THE YEARS, THERE HAVE BEEN THOUSANDS OF SIGHTINGS OF BIGFOOT.

"IN 1999, A MAN WAS DRIVING TO VISIT SOME FRIENDS IN OREGON.

"HE PULLED OFF THE ROAD TO GET SOME SLEEP IN HIS CAR. HOURS LATER, HE WAS AWAKENED BY A LOUD CRASH."

CRASH!

"WHEN THE MAN TURNED ON THE HEADLIGHTS, HE SAW A BIGFOOT STANDING IN THE ROAD.

"THE BIGFOOT STARED AT THE MAN FOR A WHILE AND THEN WALKED OFF INTO THE WOODS.

"A FEW DAYS LATER, IN THE SAME AREA, A WOMAN SAW A BIGFOOT CATCHING FISH IN A STREAM."

DOES ANYONE KNOW WHAT KIND OF ANIMAL BIGFOOT MIGHT BE?

SOME SCIENTISTS THINK IT MIGHT BE AN UNKNOWN TYPE OF APE OR BEAR.

"OTHER SCIENTISTS THINK IT MIGHT BE A CREATURE THOUGHT TO BE **EXTINCT**, LIKE *GIGANTOPITHECUS* OR *PARANTHROPUS*.

"BIGFOOT COULD EVEN BE A CREATURE LIKE A GIANT SLOTH."

"AFTER JERRY CREW FOUND THE FAMOUS FOOTPRINTS, A MAN NAMED RAY WALLACE SAID HE HAD MADE THEM AS A JOKE.

"AFTER THE FAMOUS FILM WAS TAKEN BY PATTERSON AND GIMLIN, A FRIEND OF THEIRS CAME FORWARD TO SAY THAT THE CREATURE WAS HIM DRESSED IN AN APE SUIT."

More Bigfoot Stories

- **Albert Ostman and the Bigfoot Family**
  In 1924, Albert Ostman was near Lund, British Columbia, Canada, looking for an old gold mine. At his camp deep in the woods, he awoke one morning to see that his pack had been emptied and some of his food was missing. He assumed that a bear had visited his camp. For three nights, the visits continued. The fourth night, Ostman tried to stay awake in his sleeping bag, waiting for the animal with his rifle. However, he fell asleep. He was awakened when someone picked him up and carried him out of camp. He found himself trapped inside his sleeping bag. The creature took him to a bigfoot camp. The next morning, he found himself with a bigfoot family, including an adult male and female and two children. A few days later, he managed to escape from the family and make his way back to civilization, where he told his story.

- **The Maine Ridge Monster**
  In 1988, a father and son went fishing in stream in a remote backwoods area of Penobscot County, Maine. As they hiked along the stream, they felt that someone was watching them. On the way back to their truck, they stopped to rest at an abandoned cabin. On the table was an old journal in which someone had noted sightings of a "ridge monster." A few hours later, on the hike back to their car, the father and son came face to face with a huge bigfoot in their path. The creature disappeared into the woods. The father described it as more than 8 feet (2 m) tall and weighing an estimated 500 pounds (227 kg).

Glossary

attacked (uh-TAKD) Tried to hurt someone or something.

evidence (EH-vuh-dunts) Facts that prove something.

exists (ig-ZISTS) Lives or is real.

extinct (ek-STINKT) No longer existing.

folklore ((FOHK-lor) Stories or traditions that have been handed down among people.

Gigantopithecus (jy-gan-toh-pih-THEE-kus) An extinct ape that lived from one million to as recently as 300,000 years ago.

hoax (HOHKS) Something that has been faked.

legends (LEH-jends) Stories, passed down through the years, that cannot be proved.

missionary (MIH-shuh-ner-ee) A person sent to another country to tell people about their religious beliefs.

nocturnal (nok-TUR-nul) Active during the night.

Paranthropus (puh-RAN-thruh-pus) An extinct species of hominid, or manlike animal, that lived around 2.7 million years ago.

plaster cast (PLAS-ter KAST) A mold of something made from a mixture of sand, water, and lime that hardens as it dries.

sensation (sen-SAY-shun) Something or someone that is very good or exciting.

Index

Websites

Due to the changing nature of Internet links, PowerKids Press has developed an online list of websites related to the subject of this book. This site is updated regularly. Please use this link to access the list:

www.powerkidslinks.com/mons/big/